watery through the gaps

for dad,
for teaching me not to discard what is broken, but to
piece it together, with polish and grit, to live anew, as
poetry.

her own salt

i.   there is an ocean between us—
what i mean by that is i have spent
my days collecting rocks in my pockets
and calling them *sea glass*; i have
named the dust of my bones *sand*
and tried to conjure the precise texture of sea foam,
but i have come up empty and dry.

ii.   it's been too long since i've stood at the shoreline;
even so, i find the ocean's voice
in the gray stillness of the morning—
the way faucet water runs over
my knuckles reminds me of
how i once held the waves
and stood swaying and solid
on their grainy underpinning,
listening to her song, trying to learn
to be and be.

iii.   the first time i visited the sea,
my mother stripped me to my diaper
and held my pudgy, soft skin to the water,
let the waves lick and lap over my legs
until they scooped me up
without warning and carried me away—
somehow, i think
i've been there ever since;
somehow, i think
the ocean has wrapped my heart in seaweed,
in sand, in breeze,
and called me her own salt.

by adeline gray

watery through the gaps

poems by emma blas

foreword

i should tell you these are the songs of the sea. that if you hold a seashell to your ear all her secrets will come spilling forth. but that would be a lie.

the songs of the sea aren't contained, they are infinite, ancient, world-wide wisdom; they are everywhere. they are ours to treasure if we can just find a way to listen. listen for them in the roar of the waves, the way the sea spittle foams and fizzes, the melody of the rain, the quiet mist; feel them in the sweat, the blood, our tears.

these poems were written against the backdrop of an increasing climatic emergency, a global pandemic, and the unfolding of a personal grief. what started as translating the warning i heard in the sea's rage, turned to witnessing the planet redressing the great balance and my own struggle to adapt to life's inevitable cycle into loss.

what i initiated as a listening, an invitation into dialogue with the great waters, became me walking down to the water's edge in search of comfort. i find i am lighter when i leave.

so, i look for her in the morning dew, in the sea mist rolling in, the rivers and the lakes, because i feel she is hope. i want to follow that path back to her, where she waits with a smile, asking "what kept you?"

may these songs echo to something deep within you, and reconnect you with the great waters within. listen to her song and trust the current. despite the terrifying tug of the undertow, we are exactly where we are meant to be.

contents

i.   what the sea heard

17   shadow walker
18   sometimes we have to get tangled to find a single thread
19   in the shadows
20   feather weight
21   at least 27 reasons why i cannot be loved
22   all those little big things
23   today i can't do the work
24   dark fawn
25   i want to…
26   when tides rise, islands sink
27   cry-baby
28   to ripple
29   how high will i rise?
30   from water, to stone
31   the edge of moonlight
32   the good old days

ii.   what the sea saw

39   worn hollow
40   too big to swallow
41   candy box
42   easy burnt rust
43   the glimmering
44   mountain flanked
45   bare and bold, as sand
47   the flag-less pole
49   the old man
50   thin and dry and dull and paper
52   i don't have to believe in jesus to know that i will be saved
53   this poem wants to be a bit savage

iii.   what the sea knew

59   for the indian cheetah, the sumatran rhino, the chinese
       paddlefish and all the other species that went extinct last
       year, when climate change wasn't happening...
60   madreselva
61   7 minutes
62   force of nature
63   still
64   a house built on fat lies
65   dare to burn
66   all the things that can break
67   how to hold a life?
68   i am the river running itself home
69   together, but alone
71   waterrise
72   even crows are mothers
73   blue
74   this isn't about…
75   the edge of sunset

iv.   what the sea said

81   some days i go to church
83   i'm always holding two ends
84   the wish and the penny
85   showing off the light
86   i am not the maker
87   slip and slide
88   salivate
89   a moment in time
90   things which at first glance are not beautiful

v.	what the sea did
95	he says he wants to fuck me
97	the moment is shedding its skin
98	effervescent
99	asymmetry of the storm
100	always
101	arm's-length
102	little dead bodies
103	first earth
104	war cry
105	in-sight
106	food for the moon
107	a moth's lament
108	finding the way back home
113	closing poem 'ornithophobia'
115	acknowledgments
117	about the author

~ what the sea heard ~

we have become those two old friends
finishing each other's sentences,
understanding all the exquisite pain of a beautiful life
in a look,
side-by-side, we talk the night away;

the night talks back, i am shook
awake, to being an endless, ancient
inconsequential thing again
in a world of single-stem vases humming, i-i-i-i-i
i am back to choking on the browning leaves
discarded
when each vase becomes an echo;

i want to shake them awake,
as the night once woke me,
but i stop, pause my hands, know
it was only because i am now empty
of echo, emptied of me,
that i can hear the hum
of my own wave on the shore; -
could even know what a friend is
by looking myself in the eye;

and so i wait for you to wake,
wait until we can talk,
until there is no night or day,
until there is no me absolute yet filling
with all the forgotten,
because there is no me or you,
until we are just a sentence being
finished by the other,
letting ourselves be moved
by the lullaby of the night.

shadow walker

every empty vessel
            is a gap begging to be filled.
     a tea cup,   a wine glass,
     the silence hanging two curtains between
     us,   the soft hollow dent,   on the other side
     of the bed;

if you do not   own your   darkness
it will snap,   hungry,   bite   the fingers
     from   any hand
trying to drop in a penny,
          a   hole   baying
          and   aching
          and   sucking
all   the lamentations   walking the known
       and unknown   world;

the glass sings, when the finger,   wet and
firm,
     circles the emptiness, without rushing;

the glass sings, whether the glass,
     is empty   or full.

sometimes we have to get tangled
to find a single thread

i listen at the edges of birdsong,
ears strain to bleeding,
hoping to hear the trill
"you belong",

all the decisions i have ever made
lay tangled in my lap,
i am trying to follow a thread,
to make the next one lead
to a place where i am meant to stay,
but i keep losing my spot.

in the end,
the crow will fly back to its nest,
and it will be carrying a piece of corn
left by the harvester,
or maybe it won't,
and the chicks will or maybe won't go hungry;

either way i will still be here
watching it all,
with my bag of ifs and nots;
either way i will snag
the unravelling,
on a hang nail, i have refused to cut
or, i will knot myself
a blanket of messy today,
lean into
this place called home.

in the shadows

today i don't quite know
what to do with such a vast,
great thing as the sky,
any more than i knew what to do
yesterday, with such a tiny,
boundless thing as the heart;

i wonder what will happen,
if i see a wolf in the clouds,
or the world turns to violet,
or if the gull is not perched,
prince of his rock, when i pass by;

this heart drops like coins
in a puddle, at the question
of tomorrow, yet somehow, still
can fit silently into the pocket of my throat,
folded neatly into a napkin,
it is ready to mop up any mess made
if, or rather
when, it breaks,

my own voice
has stopped to echo back to me,
and it is that sound of silence
with the sky wrapping
itself around me,
all violet, vast,
and unquestionably broken,
that is me.

feather weight

i feel weighted to this place
like any other,
to you, as to others before,
like i have ash in my shoes,
and i don't know if it is me
burning things as i go,
or just that pebbles turn to sand
in my palms, until
like an autumn leaf,
i am gauzy,
the wind blows me away
through the hole in my pockets
i never quite get around to sewing shut.

at least 27 reasons
why i cannot be loved

i can count the reasons why not to
until i run out of fingers,
peel back the skin
and begin counting bones.

starting with my fingertips,
i have reached the carpals
still finding excuses
as to why i cannot let you love me,

i am throwing up walls
like an umbrella to a storm,
trying to turn back the tide
when the moon is fat and full,

trying to hold back a river
that was born to run,
trying to cage a heart
that was bred to beat wild.

all those little big things

it's said to be
the strongest muscle
in the body;
picture it,
all the work it does
at wagging,

        and biting itself back,
       and all those little big things
        it has to hold underneath,
        secrets the size of shears
         that could sink a ship;

seven pieces of silver,
stuffed in a purse and saved,
to pay the ferryman,
tied down tightly with fear
knotted into rope,

        swept under canvas,
     we hide all the pieces of ourselves
       we're afraid to be known
        by the outside world;

i would rather cut it into slices

         to count the rings

that a true word leaves,

         than watch it bloat

in my mouth,

         swollen in misuse.

today i can't do the work

i can't ask *how are things?*
what if you ask me back?
i don't know how to tell you
that i am a goldfish
swimming in a solid bowl,
or a fly trapped in amber,
somehow i am tree
and sap, bowl
and goldfish,
young and also
so old,
all these things
and also
none.

i can write words,
maybe even some you want to read,
or write a dialogue
retelling my own story;
but how do i do that underwater?
the ink bleeds,
fins or tail can't grip a pencil,
without earth, the roots float
on the surface,
without skin, the water
is washing me dry.

i want to swim to safety
but i don't know which way is land
and i am too afraid to call out,
for what if my body finds a new way to breathe
and jumps out
through my open mouth?

dark fawn

rinsed in dark rivers
this fur, once white
is now mottled sable;
though it becomes me
and this soft, sensuous face,
my thoughts stain
the snow outside,
blood dropped
by sacrifice.

i wait wild eyed
by lake's side,
wish for a tide
wash me away,
too caught in the bullrushes
of my past to see
there is always
an opposite shore
containing me.

i cannot bolt
for i have been hobbled
by indecision,
and in truth,
have nowhere to go,
i must drink my own blood
to be whole.

i want to…

i want to call you
periwinkle,
though i don't know
if that is your name;

all i know
is that a stream runs
beneath your feet,
and pools in rocks
where the birds
and the lizards,
maybe even the fairies
come to drink
on a midsummer's eve.

maybe i will lie down
beside it a numb goddess,
and wake a woman
flawed, yet forgiving
of myself.

or maybe i will be taken
by the selkies
whilst i slumber,
wake to find myself
breathing under water,
flippered.

come what may,
i want to wake
fearless.

when tides rise, islands sink

i have floated as an island,
untethered by bridges burned,
smoked until all the boats
char down to fish bones.

the people hold a light to the water
think it a spectre,
but yes, an island can move;
it treads water,
yet can risk it all
on a cresting wave.

finally, i breach your shores.
will you welcome me,
a refugee from a land
that is no longer safe for me?

or will you leave me
to stand in line,
waiting for my number to be called
with only sand in my pockets?

cry-baby

the act of crying is an allowing,
a leeching; stagnant hearts, bleeding
to be drawn back into something
greater than, yet, also of, itself.

one lone tear drops with the force
of gravity, with the force of wanting,
to join, to be, perpetual;
to be immortal glass.

to ripple

in the end,
isn't it all about learning
how to let ourselves
r i p p l e,
instead of being parted,
                    -cleaved,
each time somebody
passes through?

how high will i rise?

how high will i rise for this tide
knowing, as i do,
that it will take me with it
and i may never find this 'home'
again?

how many nights will i lay
listening for the moon, as i do,
bid me run with her
and be gone so many days
that my feet forget the feel of dew
upon their soles
again?

how many suns will i follow
searching for its gold, as i do,
finding it already glimmers
right here, right now
at the bottom of this deep blue,
my deep blue soul
again?

from water, to stone

my mind runs now
with the tide,
a flightless bird
it will not settle,
on any place
for any time.

i will not allow the crows
to make their home here,
their caw is enough
to scare stones
from their resting,
for they will pick the bones
from the weak, where they stand;

i had one once,
on my shoulder,
looking back, unnerving
those who try to follow.
just a look, from crow's beady eye
is enough to turn a man to water,
to run like a river for the sea.

but there is a crop of rock,
in the middle of the ocean
where a being, more mer,
than man, turns back
from water
to stone,
to tether this wild mind,
this wild me.

the edge of moonlight

sunlight, the enchanter
beckons
with long fingers of gold,
that whisper silently
"follow".

i trace along the edge of moonlight,
as it unravels
to pool in my palms.
i pocket those silver coins
for the long journey
along night's river,
home, to the living;

i will swap this raven's call
for a ride
on the wing of a gull,
let this voice soften
salt and brined,
to a howl for the moon.

the old good days

i would sit draping her pearls
around my thin neck,
watch how her marcasite brooch,
and her one-diamond ring
caught the light,
shaking her snow globe on the dresser
i would imagine the snow swirling around us,
eternal, maternal,
comforting, snow.

i can shake that snow globe
until my arms burn
but she is not standing beside me,
she is not loving me,
and it's been so long since she was
and since she did,
and my mind has sort of broken off in chunks,
not quite like how a landslide crumbles
or the way a glacier shears off,
but like a continental plate shifting,
        though it might also be drifting,
                            away.

i think it's the way a tree would sacrifice a limb
to save the greater good
of itself,
and myself
is going the same way
shaking off old beliefs,
        at least i hope that is what is falling.

she will never be one i shake off,
but i can't stop seeing us standing there
together in sepia,
only now we are showered
by multi-coloured
plastic snow,
and i want more than anything
for it to be the good old days
again, for it to be more
than a memory.

~ what the sea saw ~

i wonder does the moon look down
onto an earth crawling in ants
does it watch as we cut off little bits of leaf
chop the bodies in our path into parts
we can more easily carry back to the hive?

except the body parts are forests
and marshes and reefs
and we are drilling the gold out
from right under our nests
just to send a ship to mars

far out of moon sight
it will bring back rocks
we can roll as dice
with lord elgin's marbles
africa's diamonds
and all the other stones we don't need
to eat or breathe
and yet we sit here sucking thumbs
crying because we still want m o r e

only we can't be ants
surely we aren't smart enough?
we don't know how to collaborate
how to use what we have
or how to share
we just chew chew chew
voracious
waiting on the moment
to start eating the moon.

worn hollow

i am a path worn thin
by the passage of a thousand feet
passing by,
me; a hole, worn hollow
by the insistent lowing of the waves,
either way you can run your hands
along my body,
smooth, a little dusty perhaps
depending on the tide,
stop for a moment
where your finger slips, fitting
a soft little nook,

and after all isn't that the sum of a day,
perhaps even
a life?

too big to swallow

i have a fat tongue
swelling with a force,
tidal, or is it that water
is leaking from my blood,
to thicken, cornflour added
spoon by spoon,
until it fills my mouth.

when it is fat, as it is now,
i mumble a thank you
around and through it,
although mostly silently
to some angel, or demon,
that it is too big to swallow
and choke on,

and somehow i can sit
at the table and chew
through this whole meal,
despite the gravy
being lumpier
than the words in my mouth,
despite it being big enough
to float on,
despite losing the way
to taste a life.

candy box

i have been giving myself away,
handing pieces out
as if it were candy,
rather than limbs
from a broken tree,

i have no leaves left
to shield myself,
and i stand naked
before you.

i am tinder,
snapping easily,
in rough hands,
but i will not burn
if you offer me a place
beside your hearth.

you stare,
instead of covering my shoulders,
instead of giving me pieces
of you.

i realise, too late
there is a season
of giving,
and receiving,
a season to fall.

my breath rises,
steam
in the cold.

easy burnt rust

i want to write a poem that is easy,
that may even say some soft words to itself,
in a sunday-afternoon-40's-jazz
kind of listening, slow dance
in the kitchen, found in the moment,
into letting go long sigh, kind of easy;

but how does one write of that kind of peace,
when the ocean is having to teach me
what the body does to breathe?

small blessings that the weather today
is not as all-hell-broken-loose
as i feel inside;
i want to believe this day will be the rust
staining the insides of a conifer,
to make it glow against the setting sun,
for without it, without hope, it's just burning,
and can easy, once singed, ever
grow back?

the glimmering

there is a pink hint
of a sun trying to set,
as there is the scarlet trace
of a monster within me;

just as the camera can never quite
capture what the eye can see,
so too, the eye cannot grasp
what truly lies beneath.

a cerise disc now
the sun melts from view,
but it will keep burning
longer than our eyes can hold,
what else stays aflame so,
burning out of view?

lust can turn us into crackers,
to be crushed or cracked open;
life can reduce us
simmering to black tar;

sometimes reaching for others
we leave a greasy stain,
and in that slick
we see confirmation

that we should have stayed
more safely contained,
and we chew back the many arms
of the leviathan
to only two.

mountain flanked

here i stand looking down
a concave 2000 metre emptiness,
that wants me to know its hunger,
how daring to stand alone
has cost it from the bones,
first by giving rib back to adam,
it has gone on hollowing from then;
i want to scream into the slurry,
that i can hear the rumbling,
to hold on, because rain is coming,
but my toes are peeking at me
from all the way down at the bottom,
i no longer know if this is a mountain
or a storm i called in from across the ocean,
throwing words into my open mouth
i try and catch snowflakes
to nourish myself.

bare and bold, as sand

i bared my breasts to the ocean.

without blinking,
or missing a beat,
it took all of me in,
in wide-eyed regard,
kept rolling and churning
and i kept standing,
bare and seen.

bend me over bow,
as the biggest wave
breaks with force,
this need to feel a ship
rolling within me;

let the delight be,
in turning a pebble
over in my fingers,
in feeling it weathered
smooth,

let the space within me
fill instead,
with the sound
of their falling,-
of their rising,

let me watch watery
through the gaps,
as stones roll
with the drag,

and stay instead
anchored to the knowing,
that they will do this
even when broken into sand,
and the sand does not end there,
it will dampen and dry,
mix and churn,
and spread with others
whilst remaining in itself bare,
it will let itself be taken bold
by the ocean's design;

i cannot un-see this.

i cannot un-know this
way of the rocks,
and i cannot re-cover myself,
for i cannot stop wanting
to be known
as a woman
who is strong enough
to crumble
into sand.

the flag-less pole

flag-less, rope
slack and without purpose,
clacks an s.o.s. alarm;
this rattle has no need,
this twang of jute
against metal,
built, to save lives,
no longer guards the people
from the currents,
        (or was it the currents from the people?)
it was built to send a signal,
now it can only clack, clack,
dot dot dot dash…

if it can still bring people
to its attention,
it will have done its job
and sent a message,
even if only its own prayer
to be noticed, to exist
within the circle
of disinterest;

but it goes unheeded,
and as the wind picks up
across the sands, that could
on another day, be called peaceful;
the flag-less pole's panic
is palpable, shuddering in the wind,
clack dot dot DOT dadadada-dasssshhhhh,
tethered useless,
as it is, to a flag-less pole.

let me tell you, flag-less pole,
i heard you calling,
and i stopped to watch,
and listen for a while
to your song with the sea,
and the sand,
with the leaves of the trees,
the terns and the curlews,
the pigeons and the bees,
and yes, me.

the old man

he sits in the old stone circle
breaks the silence of the waves
with a radio
as the voices crackle
arriving disembodied
the lichen continues to breathe
and breed
it is growing over his hand
with every hour that rests on his stick
his cap turns slowly from white
to yellow
one day
he will match the sun
when his bones
sigh out like the algae
bound in service to the lichen

for now, he will stay steady
guarding the coastline
with his unwavering gaze
and we will know we also exist
by meeting it

he has turned to watch me
and i wonder how far he has walked
here alone
to behold me like this
in witness
and if i ask him
will he let me join him
walking the long way home

thin and dry and dull and paper

i find i am becoming thin,
and it is more than paper thin.
but tell me,
what is thinner than paper
whilst still wanting to be a surface?
what can be erased and yet
still be written upon?

some days you can see through me,
a sheet of an untouched bible
left forgotten in a hotel room drawer;

i am craving a different wisdom
that on other days, is crisp
as fresh onion,
fleshy under the brown paper-bag lining,
for the carrying
has peeled it through,

walls can pass through the eye of a needle,
the sound of your own crumbling
passing right through
too,

the other side is
[where?]
there
also here
also me
[when?]

once i was more than a wisp,
before all the veils
were membranes
holding tight,
before the sound of pins, dropped
onto the finest, tiniest
of thin finger tips
[how?]

before a drop of water
washed the words away,
before a drop of water
brought them back to life,
[when?]

i don't have to believe in jesus to know that i will
be saved

it is a thousand miles of sky
from night, to cool white, then grey,
black to night, and into
blue.
the whole damn way the trees are breathing
into the space beneath the clouds;

and if they keep breathing
all hot, eggs-boiling-dry
in the pan hot, all sandpaper stripping
at that walls hot, all shower turned up to max
can't open the windows, -hot,

if they keep breathing that throaty deep,
gravel up from a chest that can't get enough
air,- deep, and a back of the mouth that's gone dry
wanting to do that old type
of easy, deep, naive breathing
we used to do, before we started holding
in our breath when the phone rang,

when clouds had the depth to hold a daydream,
when they weren't just wallpapered sky;

then, finally, the walls will sweat
instead of me,
something will break free
and someone will call my name,
i will turn and i will smile
for i will know i once was named.

this poem wants to be a bit savage

if i was a poem
i'd probably be a rambling haiku,
a small bright flower
protruding from a crack in the tarmac,
all clumsy limbs
lanky in apology
at the mercy of the seasons,
in part, the rest implied
or hidden away
beneath heavy feet,
in politeness, kindness,
in trying to effort itself succinct
yet spilling over myself with too many syllables,

at first, structure reassures,
requirements to be scratched off a list,
breathing relief at meeting *criteria*,
yet somewhere in the middle,
there are too many containers,
feet become bound, growth stunts,
roots constrained, *on purpose,*

don't be tempted to think this poem needs rescuing,
it's just that it wants for a different form,
to be
poignant,
and all over again,
she is back to wanting to be versed
free, left to ramble,
to go back to being
a bit savage.

~ what the sea knew ~

in the morning i am a translucent thing
made of mostly air and water
the ocean breathes into my mouth
wave by wave
pump by pump
blow by blow
until again
i take on form
a figurine etched
in sand
grain by grain
moment by moment
thought by thought
poured through the hourglass
into the great dark lagoon below

for the indian cheetah, the sumatran rhino, the
chinese paddlefish and all the other species that
went extinct last year, when climate change
wasn't happening...

a house fly has given in
to surveying the ceiling from its back
upon the window ledge,
vacant eyes rattle in his empty head,
or at least they do in my imagined
sweeping him onto the floor;

but the air is still and thick as cold syrup
and instead i want to lie down too,
look up and see the world
with my two eyes as fly's dried up five
once used to see,
i want to pass some of the day away
giving into the despair;

fly has nothing but patience,
but he will not cry for me,
and i cannot resuscitate him with salt water,
sweat, or the sea,
or my tears,
or my tears,
or my tears;
it is too much to be bearing witness.
something is always dying
and i am a useless appendage
wanting to be part of a whole body,
to be part of the connected,
to be part of the all.

madreselva

honeysuckle licks around me,
a wild-mother
slithering on a warm wind,
she draws the night down
into her sticky arms,
where she opens her sweetest parts,
her gift for the dawn.

i am the witness,
my mouth thick
with the richness of her scent.

and i am also the night,
holding her as tight
as she holds a hummingbird
fluttering dizzy, to be close
to tasting her.

7 minutes

i can hold the sun
in my palms, yet
still belong to the dark side
of the moon.

it is here, in the ocean
i am with them both,
the light above
the dark below,
together;

when long shadows pass,
and the light begins to shine
from the creatures in the deep;
when everything is upside down,
i am with them both,
though they do not meet
except in me.

is this who i am?
am i the sea?

in her waters
can i blend?

salt and water,
to calm the boiling
of a once beautiful
mind.

force of nature

gliding through water i gasp and cry in surprise,
silks ripple, until parting. yet and yes, also wonder, at all
out of water, i see,
the bird heaves naivety of gills,
lurching through the air. amphibian maybe, i be;
i wonder then, yes maybe, it be time
whether this earth to return to water,
is my element, let connective tissue melt
for i too lumber in the fire of words,
clumsily on land, i flood into ocean,
i long for the grace for i cannot turn back
of the water, slide into ether
over my body, without evaporating
in and through, my toes. all the waters of the world.

still

i am woken by the gathering outside my window
the sparrows are louder, still

what part of alone is with?

all day the lemon tree is busy with fruit
the bees' feet stay dusted with pollen
going from here to there
and there to here

what part of close is open?

the swallows flit and turn before dusk
bats make me dizzy going this way then that
yet i haven't seen a rock turn to sand

what part of stop is moving?

the house is still standing
i am here, still

what part of me isn't stone?

a house built on fat lies

my thoughts fly without pause
turn in on themselves
noisy drones
circle the middle east
swat at big flies
disturbing our idea
of peace
and order
package it up with a slogan *(fat lies)*;-
'we can sell this; they'll buy it in the millions!'

somewhere somebody is staking it all
on a house of cards
and here i am, a domino
standing apart
bottom heavy, i fill my boots
with all the plastic
i can gather from the paths
and the beaches
coax sustenance from the soil
say no to all the long-haul flights
tying the world up in knots
but a disembodied
finger somewhere, grotesque
plays a video game
with my planet
with my life
and i am reeling, i will tumble
in the end
we all fall
down.

dare to burn

i'm remembering all the things
they told me not to do,
of how my face would stay that way
if the wind changed,
(it never did)
whilst the wind is a constant,
it has always been changing,

i am realising that all the parts of myself
i thought were burning,
were just me standing in a forest
lighting a cigarette,
daring it to burn.

but does anything even mean anything anymore,
when you've seen the fire blaze on the mountain,

when we understand that we could all end up
being the glow against the cloud,
rather than the fire itself,
if we were to always do what we are told.

today i won't light the candle
just to feel i am the witness of something,
today i will sleep with my face still made
and on purpose
forget to lock the door.

all the things that can break

a bough
a wing
a spine
a neck
a glass
a heart

physical, tangible
things.
but what of those we cannot see?

ideas, concepts, constructs.
dreams.
beliefs.
trust?

a spirit can break,
a life, so flimsy, wavering, can end,
yet even collecting up
all the little moments of pause,
how the breath holds at
                              i love you,
how the heart holds at
                    it's over,
would it become a break?

for our time line persists
still deeper than the spirit,
deeper till the soul;

my broken bones can be counted,
the years, weighed;
but can we measure its wholeness,
can we break a soul?

how to hold a life?

it is difficult to hold
this human skin,
that flickers and ripples
like the river.

---

it is easier to hold a river
than this human skin
that flickers and ripples
writhing like water,
to run through my fingers.

---

i can no longer
hold the human experience
within this skin,
for it ripples and flickers
and runs from me
as if a river.

---

i have never tried
to hold something
so fluid as a river,
yet it feels more in my reach
than trying to grasp
what it means to be human.

---

i am the river running itself home.

i am the river running itself home

it has rainbow silk sails
for iridescent scales
that billow and slip
between my coarse fingers,
it snags, yet continues running
away, from me,

now the river is a gazelle
running its right to freedom,
dashing, and splashing
through the plains,
whilst a lion's mouth waters
hot freedom,
to spill blood
with her jaws,

now the river is a gazelle
is a snake,
a lion might go hungry
or the gazelle may stumble,
and all the while
she will coil and squeeze
until something breaks,

now the river is a gazelle
is a snake, is a spider
who lost a leg
running for its life;
the spider could grow back a leg
the snake may shrug off its skin
the gazelle might run faster
the river might stutter and slow
but it will end up, we
will end up, running together
to the sea.

together, but alone

i walked for a while with the sandpipers
not mirroring their furtive meander
as they scuttled in and away
from tide, beast and man
i walked with purpose
for i was racing the sunset
and had little time,
after a while
they became accustomed to my stride
and were no longer fearful of my shadow
i remained enchanted by theirs,

and when i stopped to admire the sun
continuing her decent
they passed bravely by me
in fact, one ventured so near
i could have reached down
to stroke her lovely head
were she not bill down, sifting the sand
for morsels, left by the tide
just small enough
to fit in her lovely beak,

the bay was curved
and we found ourselves
the sandpipers and i
circling the very sun
that keeps us in orbit
as we do, a little, every day
without even lifting a finger
or a webbed toe,

i enjoyed those moments
of companionship between us
whirling around that great, giant orb
in such a joyful manner
that when a dog came
scaring them away
i felt such a loss at our parting
that we may never see each other again,
for whilst i tried to spin
the hands back on my watch
it could not bring them back
and our year in orbit together
proved to be, only an hour
beneath a setting sun.

that is
until…

we met again
just the following day
at the same patch of sand
as if nothing had happened
and we hadn't been hurtling around the sun
through space
107,000 kilometres per hour
together
but alone.

waterrise

time has been playing tricks on me,
turning to water
to trickle through my fingers,
or through twists
and the snap
of a serpent's jaws
it flows in all the rivers at once;

i am gasping for air,
a fish
on a dried-up river bed
wondering when the rains will come
and if they can flow backwards,

what is the opposite of cascade?

a waterrising?
is this what we see,
what we follow
when we are beckoned
by the last siren,
to the water under the earth?

even crows are mothers

the crow's squawk was the cry of a baby,
it pierced me to realise
even crows are mothers,
even crows have wombs,
closed fists, hidden beneath their wings,
or at least something as much a womb
in principle, as mine;

i hear in the cry, that they too
know hunger,
know scratching,
know bare earth,
know biting at hang nails, -
know they too will peck scraps,
peck flesh,
peck answers,
never stop sifting the putrefied spoils
for flashes of hope,
allow themselves too
to be blinded by it;
and they go on laying eggs
wishing they didn't have to harden
outside their body,
wishing they had more than sawdust
and their own spittle,
to build a nest.

blue

i woke in the sea mist
and the bamboo was silent,
but for the birds using it as a home.

i coloured my days
in the blues of the skies,
the surge of the waters
and the moon reflected
on the tide.

i will look for a place
less cold than the silent
edge of a knife,
to hollow the days
into feathered nights;

i am an offering
at the water's edge;
the cup, and the thimble,
the thirst, and the flood.

this isn't about….

her, or you,
or even him,
it's not about blue or green,
that it ebbs and flows,
or that it comes in waves,
it's about it being water,
it's about it being wet
yet never able to quench a thirst,
it's about me being me,
always swimming,
trying to turn an ocean to a lake,
it's about that ocean being also sea,
and the sea being the only thing
that can turn my legs to jelly,
it's about trying to find the shore,
and my legs turning to tail
when i reach it,
it's about trying to keep
my head up,
about trying to keep
taking a breath.

the edge of sunset

i followed sunset to the end of the world
searching for the birth of a rainbow,
it was a beginning, of sorts,
for i found instead, the end
of all my excuses,

it wasn't a crumb i laid
to follow back
in every willing step,
but a knot i untied
pass by pass,
i unspun myself
yet i did not leave myself behind,

it was so beautiful to be just me,
the wind, and the waves crashing below,
under a vast sky alive with sparrows,
they shifted and switched above,
and i beneath,
wishing for only one more thing in my life
than this perfect moment,-
to rub myself out at the edges with sunset
to blur with the sky
and the sea
to unravel into the wind
and the sparrows
into knowing and unknowing
joining with the edge of sunset.

~ what the sea said ~

there are many words
that do not translate
into human tongues,
but it is this one
that tells of how we all live
in an understanding,
in a conversation,
of how each footprint
has equal right
to mark the sand,
be it ever lightly so
or pressed deeply,
that the earth wants most to teach us;

the sea will wash over each
as indiscriminately,
as benignly,
as indifferent,
as tender,
as another
the hour we cease to be;

the sea needs no tongue
to speak,
though we need eyes open
to listen.

some days i go to church

and by church i mean
bed   (or the forest)   (or the ocean)

you can replace church
with any temple or shrine   (or tree)
                                   (or bird song)
a soft hand on rough bark   *a rough hand on soft skin*

you can fill it with the length
of a service
the number of oms it takes
to go three times around the mala beads

once for the master
once for the guru
that once of what's remaining
for me
left
always
wanting
just a little
more

it's not that i'm over
paying it forward to men
and i cannot give them my prayers
my patience
my compliance
my understanding

it's just that i'm learning
that nobody outside
this nameless wisdom
living inside of me
can know where best
my knees should be

sap is dripping down my insides
i am a tree turned in on itself
now my bark is hanging off my back
you cannot see my rings
or my ribs
but i am breathing
and i am believing
in something
and these days
isn't that
everything?

i'm always holding two ends
(for you, angel of mine)

we came into being,
and besides this one
absolute truth
we knew for sure,
the only other thing we could ever know
with any certainty,
was that at some time
we would also come
into un-being.

and just like at 40
when we feel the first icy droplet
of the end that will come calling
trickle down the backs of our necks
and start running for our lives,
i ran for us,

to hold those two ratty ends,
those two frayed and tattered ends
together, to will them back
with these hands
that also, yes,
that also unravelled them.

we unravel it all
trying to find the other end
until it is only time itself,
the start and the finish;
still, with jelly needles
we try to stitch it together
so the middle, the long
coiling intestines of us,
doesn't fall out
onto the floor, or messy
and bloody, into our laps.

the wish and the penny

the spirit has gone far from here,
it hides in the breath
passing in and out of days,
it searches for safe passage
in the seams of cognition,
knowing trust and belief
can draw it back into this body,
can stitch the scattered whole;
a hand reaches into the fountain,
the coin it finds
so reassuringly solid, and round,
the water so refreshingly cool.

i will stand at the edge
of this world,
shake my wings off,
push hard from the bottom
of this lake
called life,
i will hold the wish
and the penny,
turn my '*luck*'
believing i am already
all the things that i want to be,
i will stand in the fountain,
my fortune, my throne,

a shape is swimming through the bile in my stomach
pushing up against the oesophagus
along the saliva dripping down my throat
until out of my mouth
through the waters,
the spirit has returned to me.

showing off the light

it is in this stark,
vulnerable, edge of winter,
where the breath itself
is holding out for spring,
that the trees g l o w,

long limbs twist,
dusted with lichen, an artist
paints on moon shine,
drawing attention
to the light side of the body,
though not in a way
that hides the shadows,
but in a way
that brings them into a partnership,
bright light green
against bark;
the poet in me wonders
how still must one be
for the lichen to settle
on my limbs,
at how much dark
must i wear
to show off the light?

i am not the maker

i picked a beautiful thing
until it was down to its bones,
laid out in front of me,
turning to the next person
i say;- "see, it is as i thought,
it *is* a skeleton beneath."

and just like the watches and motors
we took apart to understand
how they worked,
only to find we couldn't
put them back together again,
i hold only bones in my hands;

collagen and calcium,
made porous by my pecking,
i realise, to my cost,
i cannot remake muscles
or ligaments,
i cannot breathe
back the spirit
through its missing mouth.

all the time forgetting
it's not just hands and mouths
that need to eat,
but also the ravens,
and the mongoose,
also the maggots.

slip and slide

it slunk into the water
all curves
and oily feathers,
all slip and slide,
glide,
until flap
and wriggle,
a silver fish
is breaking its back
to escape the beak;
until
flipped back
into gullet,
it is swallowed
whole.
in less than a second
the cormorant is diving again,
slip, slide and glide.

salivate

the dog's tongue will be wet
until he is ready to bury himself
a bone,

it is not the sandpaper tongue
of the cat,
whose tongue will be wet
until she's ready to take herself away
to lie in the soft cushion of leaves
besides the pond
to never wake up,

your tongue will be wet
until you forget what it is to taste life,
or maybe until your legs
will no longer carry you to the water;

we miss the taste of things when we cannot smell,
everything turning to wet cardboard in the mouth,
like peas mushy from the tin
without either the taste of salt
or sweet;

will you miss the smell of things
when you let your tongue go dry?
when life then loses flavour,
are you walking dead?

a moment in time

wet sand reflects the sky
be it blue, or grey,
billowing clouds
mottle a shoreline
crisscrossed by sandpiper
and seagull feet,
hollowing out seashells
littering the beach, feasting
until they too
discard them.

the sand makes no complaint
whilst it holds all
these images and forms
for their short legacy of existence,
until it is history
rewriting itself
again.

things which at first glance are not beautiful
after sei shōnagon

something dark wriggles in a chrysalis,
it hatches, all elbows,
the drag
of wet wings
from a lake of change;

sometimes we are wearing
a part of ourselves,
saggy and lumpy, it slips from the shoulder
gone slack,
we start to   come away
from our   own   skin,
where no   turned into maybe,
into   ok,   into   yes;

barnacles huddle, stuffed into crevices,
we have such a lot to learn from them about
community,
about holding on;

we can also learn about fearing our own shadow,
though i would fear more, not casting one
for this, i am afraid
of the mist;

sometimes life does not, at first glance, seem
beautiful,
is ugly until we can peel ourselves free,
until we can allow the crows to assist
in our exquisite decay;

dandelion flowers can be so   brash,
i crave also to turn as they do
to soft fluff.

~ what the sea did ~

who are we
but a conversation
with it all,
as the water of life
passes from one to another,
as the breath passes from we to tree,
tree to me,
they drink of air
i drink of air too,
and as i drink of water
i let go
what my body cannot hold,
let others
drink of water too,

and the berries grow fat and ripe
and i am left what the birds do not need
what the squirrels cannot feed
and what is left
overflows back to the earth,

the part of me told to finish my plate,
because children somewhere are going to bed
hungry, the part that fights to know when is
full
winces at all the effort'ing
going to waste,

then i feel the river within,
remember it will always come back to me
as the stream i pause to drink from,
as the jasmine on the breeze,
as the bees and the honey, as the
trees.

he says he wants to fuck me

my legs are wide open,
for the fabric of existence
to be penetrated;
but i don't believe
a job so big,
could be done by a man.

he says he wants to fuck me,
but it seems so binary,
just ones and zeros;
micro,
fleeting,
when the universe
is so vast,
and i can be fucked
by all that is,
all at once.

he says he wants to fuck me,
but i want a lover
to *dissolve* me;
water to my salt,
fire to my air,
turning leaf to soil,
nature claiming me
back to her embrace.

if i want to be fucked,
it is by her;
and i do want
to have her
fuck my brains out,
or rather off;
senses filled until i burst,

a white dwarf,
post super nova,
spent,
returned to the galactic scrap heap,
undone.

so, it is done,
she has bitten off my head,
i am, or was
her praying mantis mate,
made obsolete
in my search for wisdom,
headless, i watch in peace.

the moment is shedding its skin

sliding a snake into the next,
scales catch the light
as they drip all over,
because the moment is never satisfied,
is already pouring into the next,
seeing the potential in everything,
is pushing you forward
but reluctant also
to let go;

have you ever seen a serpent
open its jaw so wide
to eat its prey,
slowly swallowing it whole,
how it sniffed the body first
in order to begin
at the end
with the saliva?

does snake use its own slaver
to savour
as it's going,
or is it just too busy
with the mechanics and manners
of eating?

did the moment
come into being
because it was tasted,
or because we stopped squeezing
long enough to let it
glide into our
insatiable mouths?

effervescent

we can keep splitting hairs,
into he said, she said,
you said, i said,
even down into atoms,
yet still at that level
neither would *be*
without one bouncing off the other,

without the fizz of reaction
when we mix with another,
we'd just be layers and layers of dead things,
things that once bloomed;

now we're dense and heavy
to our core,
orbiting inertly,
waiting venus rise before the sun,
thinking this one planet
is two stars;
even thinking that one is circling the other
is so meta,
so petty,
seeing those two things
happen separately
when they are everything
and nothing all at once,
hand-in-hand with all the great wonder
(including us)
that is life.

asymmetry of the storm

a tip and a tap
toe to heel,
toe, heel, heel,
arms raised
circle slow,
until a stamp
and staccato
tapping, to clap,
and the skirts
are lifting
as she turns
into a rising pitch,
feet tat tatting,
chin turned up
and facing away,
she stares death
in the eyes,
poised in perfect
asymmetry,
she holds his gaze,
his grace,
until he is forgetting
who he was,
steps soften,
the storm
passes.

always

aren't we always falling up,
with the wind filling out our sails?
always flushed with the becoming?
the calm always spreading
its anchor within,
we are growing that place
we can return to;

the waves thrash,
though we will feel them
in the way we welcome
the tender roughness
of cat's sandpaper tongue;
it keeps licking at the same spot,
a layer of skin peeling off
with every rough, wet pass,
with every rough, wet wave,
eventually we will stop to feel the swell;
we will stay in the doldrums
high on life as a kite in spring,

always.

arm's-length

i dip my bones
wanting to belong
my time here not counted
in breaths, or pounds of pressure,
this eldritch blue world
has claimed me as her own
and i itch to take off this skin,
give myself to her;

but she keeps me at arm's length,
never to reach her depths
or see the creatures she confined
long ago to be treasured secrets;
for as long as i have air and fins,
i can never stop trying to unravel
her mystery, for in the life she guards,
i find mine.

her salts preserve my soul;
i am skinned and boned.

i am reborn.

little dead bodies

splash the motorway asphalt,
indistinguishable feather or fur,
as if god in her anger,
was done with the new creations
halfway through,
this uncompleted offspring
landed on the m1
just south of st albans,
cars and lorries finish the job
smearing little bodies under their wheels
whilst people drive past mouths wide open
wondering if actually rained cats and dogs,
thinking-
it could have been us,
thinking *thank goodness it wasn't us.*

at least that's how i imagine it must be,
what else is there to do with
'report of animals',
what else is there to do when
little dead bodies now litter the road,
what else is there to do with
'dark shadows on the lungs'?

a badger full-grown, curled up like a dormouse
laying still in black and white
stiffening into rigor mortis,
something i couldn't quite name
holds four legs to the sky in defeat,
'take me back god, take me back
is the whispered prayer of every tire-scrap and lost shoe
as they play their part in my mini-mass-extinction,

when little dead bodies now line the road,
when it's already too late to make them not,
when it's already spread to the bones?

first earth

it smells like the first earth here,
how i imagine it would smell
after all the colliding and crashing,
and erupting
has cooled into a relative peace,
after promise has simmered
down to an offering,
until the earth is breaking bread with itself,
and we, part of the sweet dough inside
are scattered crumbs,
wheat without winnow,
salt from rocks and flats and ocean alike,
water pure and free;

i am eve and adam both,
mother and also child,
my bones will one day feed a great tree,
become one burst of acorns
launched into the world,
flecks of my flesh turned hard again,
and one more time i will lay down on the leaves
smelling the rain as if it was the first.

war cry

at 40 i ballooned.
each lip a great zeppelin
ready to ride into war,
i was so full
from swallowing
when i wanted to spit,
all my honey
soured,-
curdling the milk;
the sound of the word *no*
rich and round,
and new
in my unseasoned mouth,
how could i shrink back
to being a nice girl?

the magazine covers
are screaming, call me
'another shouty woman',
though we've never met,
though they haven't heard
a word
i've said,

yes, i suppose there is some truth,
for i am a woman,
and i am speaking loud
to be heard
in a world that doesn't listen,
i am speaking loudly
the planet's war cry,
but to me,
it sounds to be
the refrain of a song.

in-sight

my third eye
is a swirling, glowing orb,
glacier blue, pearlised,
an egg, a seed,
a planet in itself,
an eagle claw reaches for it
in shadow, and now
my consciousness is breaking out
of my forehead,
not in a fracturing way,
but in a hand slipping, whilst
the mouth and eyes are smiling,
until everything is midnight blue
kind of a way,
i should be terrified,
for my sanity, for my life,
as the iridescent jellyfish floats down
through the water to me,
yet when one of its giant tendrils
wrap around
i feel the greatest relief,
the gentlest peace,
i am leaning into the oldest grandmother
that has ever been
or ever will be,
i want to stay like this,
this child,
this bud,
this us,
and never float back up again.
or is it down?

food for the moon

wolf eye is watching
under the shiver of moon
no light to illuminate
yet still she sees our truth *(lies)*

fat and full
moon's come a calling
cover your eyes
but she won't hide

crow carries something in beak
i cannot tell what
but it could well be me
ragdoll arms pinned to my sides

what am i but flesh, or bone
or just emotion, bare and juicy
and thirsty
until i am boiled into pieces
a dried-up chew
nothing but food for the maggots
nothing but food for the moon

a moth's lament

i have been the wind gathering
the tall grasses to her,
the river that at first rippled
in the sunshine, then turned to sticks
and stones, building dam to leap over,
a deep lake taken to living on its surface,
i have been the bowerbird
searching bright blue adornments
so that you might notice me;

but both tortoise and crab
i have always built my own home,
carrying it on my back, heavy and mine,
caught in a cage
i am no longer the butterfly
opening its bright wings
just for you, they have faded
into a moth's autumn dust,
i am just an old stone shattering
into splinters, the diamonds within me
brighten my own eyes.

finding the way back home

she has stopped to visit me in my dreams,
instead, i find myself running up endless stairs
until i trip,
until both up and down
become equal,

without the sound of footsteps,
without the light dappling the surface,
without the being led,
how can i know which part of my body
i should send my energy to,
which part of my body can power me onward?

it seems the question is not
which way is forward, nor is it
what is up?
nor, what is down,
but where and who am i?
and can i trust myself,
will i know when i get there?
will i just
know?

life has turned in equal parts
to thriller, tragedy, comedy,
so, i invite in a softer tone
turn the script to romance, choose
to know my silent letters
reach their muse,
believe we both remember,
know that even as she lets me walk away

she is willing me
turn, turn, turn to look back,
that maybe this story was made to have a happy middle,
maybe it doesn't end how we wanted,
when we began, but it was written
wholeheartedly, and that is ok.

the waves are walking with me
it's a different form of surrender

ornithophobia

it paces,
a tail flicks,
almost irritably,
almost palpably,
left to right,
left to right,
swish, twitch,
swish, twitch,
lurch,-
an internal metronome
soundless, invisible,
yet with a mass of weight
to throw the world off balance,
a friend pushing us from falling
down the hole, to land instead
upon grazed knee, or elbow
on the pavement
and into their thick dark arms;

the sparrow in the pit of my belly, settles,
looking more closely, i see
that what i took for freckles
is lichen, my arms branches,
my stomach a dry hole
holding a nest
and birds come and go;

the hunger i could not satiate,
tiny sparrow mouths chirping for insects
all along, the cage has become sanctum,
we lean into the thick dark night.

~ t h e e n d ~

acknowledgments

i want to thank you for holding this book in your hands, if you weren't reading these words, they would be just ink on paper. you have given them life. thank you. to my rag tag bunch of poets, artists, writers, photographers, musicians and lovely humans that keep me connected and inspired in creative community, thank you for being here. i want to call out a few in particular. atulya, i am so eternally grateful for the advice and encouragement and for the roots you give me, thank you for always having something interesting to say! adeline, you always get me, and help me find my way, understanding what lies beneath, even when I don't. thank you. mare, i was all kinds of honoured by the beautiful art you created for these books, and then you read the poems to your unborn child…! thank you so much for this gift. shelly & lubomira every poet needs cheerleaders like you! for ashley-jane, mei & kat for being my earliest community and for keeping me inspired, for eliza and emily for chats and oh the beautifully crafted poems, for sally for painting me poems to wake up to, lyn! for making me think about things differently, amy kay your prompts are everything, with you i stretch myself, thank you! davia, ness & amy w you are proof to never underestimate the power of a kind and thoughtful word in making somebody feel heard. jen for not quitting on keeping this year afloat with your upbeat encouragement, conny for echoing my desires for conscious and considered poetic community, ceeg for being an all-round beautiful human being, ana y karlita gracias por aceptarme en tu hermandad creativa con los brazos abiertos (y gatos). last, though probably foremost, as both the greatest creative force and inspiration of all, mother nature, i would be wordless without you.

about the author

emma blas lives near gijón in spain. her poetry explores transitions, shifts of phase and form in the natural world. you will find her at the beach, walking through the dramatic landscape of asturias, or with her hands in the soil, trying to learn from the earth. it is these crossing points between the physical, psychological and imagined states of life that are painted in her poetry.

'watery through the gaps' is the second of five elemental, poetry books, in conversation with the natural-world. the first, 'no less wild than the wind' is available on amazon.

find more of emma's words at www.emmablaspoetry.com

Lightning Source UK Ltd.
Milton Keynes UK
UKHW010234240221
379251UK00001B/187